SOMETHING WHOLE

poems by

Jessica Rigney

Finishing Line Press
Georgetown, Kentucky

SOMETHING WHOLE

Copyright © 2021 by Jessica Rigney
ISBN 978-1-64662-650-2 First Edition
All rights reserved under International and Pan-American Copyright Conventions. No part of this book may be reproduced in any manner whatsoever without written permission from the publisher, except in the case of brief quotations embodied in critical articles and reviews.

ACKNOWLEDGMENTS

Very grateful acknowledgment is made to the presses and places where these poems first appeared:

"An Aside" appeared in *Cider Press Review,* Volume 21, Issue 2, 2019. It also exists as an experimental, poetic recording at jessicarigney.bandcamp.com.

"A body submits," "Atop rifts in windy peaks," "Once you return from ecstasies," and "Where the elbow bends" exist as one of a kind artworks of poetry hand-hammered into steel boxes as part of *Poetic Boxes,* an installation by the poet in June of 2018, in Colorado. Most now reside in private collections. A short film of their creation exists at YouTube as *Poetic Boxes: A Documentary.*

A few poems appeared in part or as previous versions at Tupelo Press as part of their July 2018 30/30 Project.

Publisher: Leah Huete de Maines
Editor: Christen Kincaid
Cover Art: Jessica Rigney
Author Photo: Jessica Rigney
Cover Design: Elizabeth Maines McCleavy

Order online: www.finishinglinepress.com
also available on amazon.com

Author inquiries and mail orders:
Finishing Line Press
PO Box 1626
Georgetown, Kentucky 40324
USA

Table of Contents

Double Velleity 1

You Have Held Up 3

Something Whole 4

Suns of No Artifice 5

Winter Burn 6

Where the Elbow Bends 7

A Repose 8

Hoopla 9

Dream Two 10

Something in the Living 11

Concerts of Inflict 12

The Skin's Instruction 14

A Body Submits 15

Loosening Effect 16

Again 18

An Aside 19

Once You Return From Ecstasies 21

Black Into 22

Unknown Are the Hands 24

Amongst Seeds Diminishing 27

Atop Rifts in Windy Peaks 28

*I mean the turbulence in my body or soul what do I know,
I wanted to soothe it . . .*

—*Friederike Mayröcker, brütt, or The Sighing Gardens*

DOUBLE VELLEITY

All sounds move out. Suspicions vivid.
At daybreak the rare stricken

Notice from a night of clear and blunt and
Pitch. Oh the stars are so very close she says.

She will not do what she has done. She'll not
Make a chain of paper. The whole lot of circlets

A fine weave of the warm. Take a red muddy road into
The plain-staked mountain unknown. Before the burn

There are degrees of unease. In scents slit open for
The rutted way she walks. She has not

Taken what she needs. Not before. Not
Yet. Perhaps the rise is wrought by

A dispense of snag hours. What stains her breast
And thigh is not the human. But the mute beast squall

Creature of a Cimmerian night. Here now crawls
A dim movement—Her four chambered heart in pursuit.

The unfold essays of sound. Their hoary ribbed wretch-bend
A summons. To combats which wait—have waited these

Long years at the mouth of a sopping road. All sounds
Reach out. In what dreams can she gather the clamor

In close about the night? What escape settles
Tender? Oh these strenuous beginnings of things.

To situate inside—unchart flesh. To alter the extant.
All sounds move. Out the wild hurtling flay of brightening

Hands. Read the sound before its widespread blaze.
Decipher a furrow before plummet and catch and

The laying down of arms and. Oh the ground she says
How it bends now. How it clangors out and out.

YOU HAVE HELD UP

You have held up
Your hands
Against need
Until your edges

Strayed.

And in the losing
Your bordered being
Is soon seized
By its unraveling.

SOMETHING WHOLE

From your mouth
Come flying
Sweetmeats—

A fine fish
Knifed lakeside
Hung from arms

Outstretched.
We are the same
You and I—

Mouths agape
Throats full at
Mere thought

Of things swallowed
And swallowing. Our
Lovely land a little

Mound of bellies grown.
And my legs part
For the finning

You the swimming
You. Me the open O
Of swallowing

Something whole.

SUNS OF NO ARTIFICE

Press your back
He says your breath into

A meadow—how a meadow
Can be worship or this

Is how it will go she says
How you'll take your time and

Not know—less has been
Made of the freshly wrought

Under he says a simmering sun
How I'll hold he tells her

Is how you'll become
The flesh of your thumb

In my mouth-clasp at the roots of
Bough sway and happenstance—you

She says are not asking any
Thing of follow or I know or

Now though you mark me
Not by tongue erotic and slid

Inside a shell—not with your hand
Middling thighs a division of—

But by a meadow in bloom under
My skin—your quiet fine tongue of

A day neatly lined with ease and
Pause and—how it will go he says

Is more thumbs on tongues
'Neath suns of no artifice.

WINTER BURN

She is certain of haze.
A mountain burns
Soundless. The distance

Requires she follow
A scent black and shining
As a seal oily and barking.

She is certain of a charcoaled
Beam's flare gleaming as a brow
Laced with sweat after. He says

It's only the fire you're dreaming.
She is certain of roar. Certain of heat
Too hot. Certain a falter will move her

To ashes weightless. What's howled
Into the chinooks comes swift across
Mountain peaks. Embers pull flames

From a throat sorry for all it said.
She is certain her heels will catch
Her knees drop. She looks to him

And hums of thermals of the eyes'
Spiral flames. She is certain of a moan
Anchored in sweet cedar hair

Skin a lather of wet. She is certain
Of all vapor rising then vanished
From her hands.

WHERE THE ELBOW BENDS

Where the elbow bends there are
Three words for the taking—one of pressure
And of pause before the breaking.
Another of backwards glances as the body
Continues forwards.

The third has something
To do with crashing or exploding—
Or the wettish lusts of hungry creatures.

A REPOSE

Pay attention. Lay yourself
Down near the door. The instant
Before it opens yields a rush of air

Imperceptible. You'll say yes again
He tells her. When a soft rabbit hunkers
Down in wet grass at midnight for the cool

Wet at its belly you'll say yes and
That you know how it feels. A picture
Of a wash of sighing and too

Much coffee makes your hands shake—
Makes you come faster than what you know
To be time and a mislay of inflections. What

Are you going to do with your hands she asks
Of him. Only a cool shower in a darkened
Room of the freshly plucked will do. Something

About a brass bed and a woman draped.
How she is draped how. The body of
A woman drapes. This mint heat is more

Than she can manage in a week with
Unyielding mechanical contraptions whining
In the night. There are more bachelor's

Buttons spilling seeds upon the walkway
Than she can cordon. You'll say you want
Nothing more than this she tells him.

But with your legs a-twitch
In a repose of indifference—you do
My dear. You do.

HOOPLA

Write the hell out of it he said
Like she was some prizefighter
Throwing herself against a body
Larger. Though she would keep
Falling forward against the wind
For the exhilaration of it yes
That's what she was trying to write—
The goddamned explosion of her chest.

DREAM TWO

Dream two is you see she tells him
As she watches him watch her hand

Move to his thigh and. Extenuating
Circumstances allow for bad weather

Allow for rain if you wish it. Allow
For the apocalyptic. For her body. Her

Body leans into his body presses into each
Bend. The receiving of a body is holy. Is

Soaked hair. Is the laundry and all
The children. Dream two is her hand

Moving rhythmic. Her mouth at his
Temple at his ear. A hand moves deftly

You see so listen she whispers
Whispers honey hey honey come

Closer now give me your—
(sound of soaked hair)

(sound of a mouth at his ear)
(sound of pressing) (sound of the holy)

And she says close yours eyes
My darling. What's to come is

Not yet known. What's to come is
The receiving is. Dream two.

SOMETHING IN THE LIVING

Something in the living
Makes dense
Air give way. Perfect
Enclosed rapture
Wrested from its tender home
Flaps up before your face
Uncareful in its hurl about.

You loose arms frantic—
Collect its shred and fail
Mastery of your guilt.

Soon its luster licks the edges
Flashes quick to blaze.
Your living risks all procedure—
For this moment
Unbehaved.

CONCERTS OF INFLICT

In my chest run flights of elk. That they
Pound roughly is not enough for me.
I've made this heart recluse in a brimmed

History. The years fan out behind every August
A deluge of careless treatment. You I have forsaken
Again and again and I know not why my feet

Upon a long road saves me from the thundering
Ransom of my soul. I dig through owl pellets
Hunting for small bones with which to pick

At my teeth. Gray stones flecked with mica find
Their way into my hands then clunk about
In this sack hung over my dark shoulder turning.

Away again and I cannot say why I wish to handle
Precious things belonging to others—why I caress
The crevice of a nicotine door jamb and whisper

Questions of a sorted nature of succumb and wend.
The length of each fingernail determines which grip
To use when carrying my broken bucket. Index

Pressed hard into thumb flesh. A cactus needle still
Sunk in the hinge of a toe—how they shimmer
In concerts of inflict. Oh that vein of exquisite

Unease—how it threads silken through a round hour.
And I know you have grown weary of my rootless craves.
But between my legs a future mounts its apex

For the ripe way in which tongues loose wry words
Meant to frighten the sovereign hold. In my nostrils
A wet heat smokes fresh cigars hand-rolled

For the occasion. And all the beating wings
Of wild birds are peeling away fast from my wall.

THE SKIN'S INSTRUCTION

It's important she says that summer
Flatten itself against autumn. That it keep

Insisting yes yes it's true yes the heat
Makes things difficult. She shows him

How her shoulders have gone. Darker still
But do you remember she looks with eyes

Wide how cold the cold is. How
We can barely stand morning until

Hot showers—press the heat inside
Our bones again he's trying. Hard

To let go a need for comforts to recall
How simple the skin's instruction. Here

She says pointing to the open. Night
Winds have come and now you've only

A moment longer before the breathing. Begins
And it'll be alright as you sleep and tomorrow

Everything changes again when
You'll see how summer. Knows how

There isn't time for fuss just enter
The day she says just enter the poem just.

A BODY SUBMITS

A body submits
its pressure—
hold   tight
yours against
(all measures)
another's.

When is lust ever
sensible?

Keep this heat
& the longed for.
What it does to a body is
make it live.

LOOSENING EFFECT

A sky without stars over a house in a yard
A red one with white trim. She loses track
Of how much longing lies beneath. Her hands

Left her body in the hot room of epiphanies
It was. The breathing. Everyone
Breathing their own rise under a sky

Without a sun. Her thigh has a loosening effect.
There are eight people you'll sleep with
She tells him but he doesn't know yet how he

A star holds the space where her eye goes each
Time if she could only lose her long leg and find
Another more even sky. He loses track of what's

Next in a night without cheese danishes.
There should have been four but now there are
None. A consequence of a loosening effect

And her eyes when they look up at him from
The bed while he hovers trying to find her
Long leg. If she could make an ache out of

A house a blue one with saffron trim and two
Bedrooms—an extra for consequences of
He's looking down at her face again each time

As she says she is going without a sun to adjust
The stars to the new way her eyes are seeing them.
To be sure the yeast for the bread blooms she says

It's essential to feed it sugar or honey. Where
The eye goes she loses track. Underneath it all
She feels him breathing the consequence of

The loosening effect and the dough will not rise
Even though the room is hot. Even though. She's lost
Both her hands forever to his white trim mouth.

AGAIN

He looks past her to the moment
when they last arrived in the same
place it's a matter of time she says
the circling back begins to become
a body palpable while carrots are peeled
and chopped for dinner at the corner
of the kitchen he's waking from the new
dream of her walking further ahead
opening his eyes again again but it's not
there where I've gone she says but back
to the house and this time all the doors
have been replaced I don't walk through
instead I am stepping back you know
like a film played in reverse remember
she asks but his eyes are closed again and
he's fallen into sleep again I'll meet you
she says I'll wait for you over here
at the corner of the field where I'm walking
in grass heavy with rain bent over
itself and that old cat we had do you
remember him he's in my arms again
I carried him all this way through thick
air.

AN ASIDE

A sun on a card on a patchwork box next to
her bed—tarot sun and two lovers not kissing just
looking at one another. She says she fell

in love with his hands first. Here's where
to insert an aside—not formally just casually. He
says it is her eyes still in the sun as she sits

on the sidewalk a heated patch. She rests inside
the tarot before she places cards into his hands shuffles
her long fingers divines using the middle one.

A middle way does not allow for asides even
on stage he looks at her cannot decide now
between her eyes which one is the lazy one

for she's closed them against his claims brought
her own body over a rise of boulders by sturdy feet.
The aside waits at the crevice where he inserts

his fingers before she even arrives. Or maybe it is
a common tree—a kind of weeping intimately. He can't
eat what she eats anymore no onion and so

breathes into her heart at the crevice at the bed by
the sun not kissing just looking at the debris. If there were
something like blood between her legs then there is where

an aside would venture its echo. She says she fell
many times while running up the stairs—no it was down
from beside the sun where she is burning. His eyes

watch her distance from the couch for the heat as she speaks
of wishing not to know the future. Melancholy always wins
she tells him—tells him with her hands how to hold

before she formally finds her feet beneath her in the middle of the stage suffering seductions. The script already belongs to her even though it only just arrived. It's a delay she says

a reluctance of the heart. He believes the moment is passed simply because the moment has passed.

ONCE YOU RETURN FROM ECSTASIES

Once you return from ecstasies
Time refashions sweet your little sufferings.

You'll walk through this world
As a drowned thing dripping
Twigs and leaves

Breathing blameless breaths
Like these.

BLACK INTO

Inside a night everything looks
Different. You hear others in the day

And know they have not
Understood the night. How

Could they when they were deep
In repose and halfway headed to

Morning under a roof pelted
By unheard rain? Thunder holds

Its hands against its mouth and asks
What the fuck am I doing? Your bare

Toes are crossed one foot atop the other
Risking the night's twenty degree drop

But you don't cover your skin for it's
Open and summered enough to know

There's no going back. You've seen
How a woman can lose a lover while turning

From a dark doorway to the road. She holds
Her pain as a balm against all other intrusions

And still begs to differ about the task
At hand—says you should have another

Drink. Yes and do you know the night
Loses its glamor as soon as it's entered?

You hear others whisper about the dark
Dust about your shoulders. How they wish

It were they who were stepping through
Black into. Yet—they won't. And cannot

Fathom how thick the air is out here where you
Have untied all the knots thrown off your skin and walked.

UNKNOWN ARE THE HANDS

You ask me of my sorrows and I
I cannot say how the wind borrows

my voice as I walk into it. I cannot
explain how I was born bereft—how

I carry what I was meant to carry. You—
you ask me why the sadness, even

as the sun flashes in my smiling eyes
and they tear before the question is

complete. And I, I cannot say how
the trees rustle away with my heart

as if it had been theirs from the first
dampened day—how my arms are meant

to open even as I weep. We hope for olives
and there they are on our plates with

crimson tomatoes sliced in half, and fresh
cheese. We ask for forgiveness perhaps

once or twice, and find an unspoken
surrender made ready to face the day.

You ask me what I might hope for
besides this and I, I am unable by virtue

of your eyes as they see me, to say
what it is I should want, beyond your notice

of my long fingers held out and trembling.
Here I have lilacs rescued from the hail

fresh coffee in my cup and thunder
in all its suddenness answering Coltrane's

ascent. I know why the starlings gather
in the tops of cottonwoods at the end

of a frayed out day, why a river never
quiets in its descent from the mountains

why a field opens itself to a spilling sky—why
the dove mourns from the roof every morning.

Unknown are the hands we will hold on a new road
in a part of town we've never seen. Here

I have new books just arrived, a poem started,
the fresh bright sun just after a spring storm.

You ask me can I find a way from this life
into another and I, I cannot say. I know only

how this sorrow is also my joy—is the pleasure
is the way I choose to wonder how it will be

in a year or ten years' time. Because never
will there be an answer arising on my tongue.

Because there are still thousands of sighs
waiting in my lungs. Because tears bide their time

as readily as the oak growing new rings.
Because I have nothing I know better among

all these things, than my unfastened heart.
Because there is not time nor a will to forget.

AMONGST SEEDS DIMINISHING

How for once I'd made a fool of myself
you began to show me what I had been
looking for—though I did not know

I had been hunting. How for once the white
hyacinths made their push up and through
my boots to split the sky between a winter's

night and spring's greedy wet lunge it was
I believe now—the last of cracked dishes. The last
of yellow yolks running beyond my hope. For me

it was how you said your ears are like a shell
and how I wanted to penetrate them in the backflow
of soft sounds you make when you are

leaning into the wide bodies of goats who know
it's best to shift a balance between hooves. How for once
I'd made a circle 'round your tender wrists

with my tongue I could see it was not the same
for you as it was for me. And I'd again make
a fool of myself for my sorrow left and still

diminishing amongst the seeds of cottonwood tendrils.
For once we know there is not an entire me inside
an entire you it is easier—still easier to let what's wanted

go.

ATOP RIFTS IN WINDY PEAKS

Atop rifts in windy peaks the falcon makes
A selection of breaths beyond her wings' rapid beats
Soon pulled taut as she dives & then exposes
Her beak & breast to maw & thrust of
Another's appetite—She dies, you see.
The giving over soon begets—

As surely as you
Walking swiftly here—towards me.

NOTES ON THE POEMS

"You have held up," "Where the elbow bends," "Something in the living," "A body submits," "Once you return from ecstasies," and "Atop rifts in windy peaks" all have a cadence loosely influenced by perpetual reading and study of Emily Dickinson's poems as they appear in the scans of their original, penciled forms at the Emily Dickinson Archive, edickinson.org.

"Something Whole" is an ekphrastic after "Big Fish Eat Little Fish" (1557), by Pieter van der Heyden, after Pieter Bruegel the Elder.

"Again" is for Columb.

"Unknown are the Hands" is after Pablo Neruda's poem, "There's No Forgetting (Sonata)," as it exists in translation by Forrest Gander, within *The Essential Neruda: Selected Poems*, edited by Mark Eisner, City Lights Books (2004).

Jessica Rigney is a poet, artist, and filmmaker. She is the author of *Follow a Field* (2016), *Entre Nous* (2017), *Within Poetic Boxes* (2018), and *Careful Packages* (2019). Two of her poems, "À la Brütt" and "Grass Began," exist as limited edition, letterpress broadsides by Wolverine Farm Publishing (2016 and 2017, respectively). Jessica was a quarter-finalist for the Pablo Neruda Prize for Poetry in 2016 and 2018.

The YouTube channel, Jessica Rigney, carries her poetic short films. Her poetic music and voice experiments live at jessicarigney.bandcamp.com. On Instagram she is poetjess, where her imagery and words, as well as announcements for new work can be found. She lives and wanders in Colorado and northern New Mexico, where she films and collects feathers and stones.

www.jessicarigney.com

www.ingramcontent.com/pod-product-compliance
Lightning Source LLC
LaVergne TN
LVHW041508070426
835507LV00012B/1422